Rock of Recovery 2
Overcoming Torment

Angie G Meadows MSN, RN
Sarah J Meadows BS

"For as he thinks in his heart, so is he..."
Proverbs 23:7

Study based on the NIV version. KJV answers are in parentheses.

A Thousand Tears, LLC
PO Box 561, Lewisburg, PA 17837
PO Box 1373 Huntington, WV 25715
enablersjourney@gmail.com
http://enablersjourney.com
http://angiegmeadows.com/
Rock of Recovery podcast
https://admin5.podbean.com/rockofrecovery/settings/feed
Angie G Meadows YouTube
https://www.youtube.com/channel/UC9l06RVhc1leng_fj8LqFPA

Table of Contents

Introduction: *6*

   Prisoners of the Flesh: No more **6**

      Evaluate 7

Principles *8*

Tormented Mind Cycle *9*

   Lesson 1..**9**

      Mental Torment Evaluation 14

Unwinding the Tormented Thinking *15*

   Lesson 2..**15**

      Spiritual Maturity Skills 18

      Thought Test Scale 19

      Mental Torment Scale 19

Offended Cycle *21*

   Lesson 3..**21**

      Signs and Symptoms of Spiritual Sickness....................23

Unraveling Offenses *25*

   Lesson 4..**25**

      Signs of Spiritual Health 27

Offense aka an Emotional Wound *30*

   Lesson 5..**30**

      How to Stop an Offense 32

      Types of Offenses...33

How to Be Blameless...*34*

   Lesson 6..**34**

      Who Needs a Boundary? 36

      Reasons to Avoid Offense 36

Yoke of Slavery...*37*

   Lesson 7..**37**

Reasons to Not Take an Offense 37
A Yoke of Slavery...39

Wounded Heart..**40**

Lesson 8..**40**
Identifying your Wounded Heart 41
Wound Identifier...41
Overwhelmed 42
Emotional Responses to A Wound...42
Bitterness Evaluation 43
Characteristic of Depression 44

Recovery from the Wounded Spirit..**47**

Lesson 9..**47**
Turning it Over 49
Boundaries with those who are Abusive or Unsafe....................49
Reframe the Wound 51

Drunk vs. Sober Emotions...**53**

Lesson 10..**53**
Drunk Emotions 53
Sober Emotions..54
Emotional Movement Quiz 55

Forgiveness **58**

Lesson 11..**58**
What Forgiveness is Not! 58
Forgiveness Steps...59
Caution..59

Freedom...**62**

Lesson 12..**62**

Moderators **67**

Small Group Rules **68**

Leadership Guidelines..**69**

Good Follower **70**

Author's Biographies...*71*

Other Resources by the authors...*72*

Introduction:
Prisoners of the Flesh: No more

Are you a prisoner of anxiety, fear, and depression? These emotions ruled my life. Surely, I didn't have mental illness: wild mood swings, mental obsessing, racing thoughts and an occasional uncontrollable fit of anger. The smallest irritations could throw me into a tailspin. These behaviors were my personality, right? I couldn't be expected to control my actions, let alone my feelings and thought life, or could I? Now what about the this "taking to my bed" and crying for hours to console myself with brooding and self-pity? This was normal for me.

On the outside, my life was a perfect facsimile of normality. This, of course, was an allusion. Appearing happily married, I had an elegant home and chased a prosperous career. However, my heart continually courted the distress of a victim's role. A never-ending search for "happiness" perpetually alluded me. Chasing the temporary and momentary reprieve from my sullenness was draining shopping, vacations, and friends. Soon the money ran out, the friends were less animated, and I could not drown the murmuring noise inside my head. Instead, work became my intense distraction to soothe the savage beast within me. It was not unusual for me to work 24-48 hours with only an hour or two of sleep. Pursuing another college degree during the day and 12-hour nursing nightshifts, left me little time to dwell on any of my past traumas or current dramas.

Burning the candle at both ends didn't serve me well. My health began to fail, and chronic fatigue ensued. One morning I was driving home from a night shift and fell asleep at the wheel. Awakened by the sound of a horn from the car behind me, I realized I had deviated left of center into the path of a semi-truck traveling 60 miles an hour. It was a narrow escape from certain death. The car was shaking from the closeness of the semi and the blaring horn rung in my ears. What was I doing?

Shaken to the core, this became a picture of my fast approaching obituary, if I didn't change my ways. Asleep spiritually and being pushed into the path of eternal death, my life was out of control. I went home. Faced my husband. Confessed my sins. Quit my job and began a journey of recovery. It has now been almost 30 years. I don't regret giving up the doctorate scholarship or the fine paying career.

Life at home, centered on Christ, focused on serving God and my family fostered an abundance of peace and joy. The road to this tranquility came from declaring war on my flesh and learning to walk in the Spirit. Conquering an aversion to reading the Bible, prayer and listening to preaching were great uphill hurdles to overcome. **Emotional immaturity and an unregenerate flesh** were no longer teaming up with Satan to defeat me. The challenge was to understand how to bring my flesh under the dominion of the Holy Spirit.

If Christ delivered Mary Magdalene from seven demons, surely, He delivered me from seventy. So, how do you comfort yourself or quiet the beast that lives within you? Alcohol, drugs, pornography, sexual promiscuity, food, games, television, shopping, vacations, friends, work alcoholism or even enabling and rescuing others, these vices are all the same. They are a distraction from your internal torment fueled by past traumas, toxic relationships and undisciplined thinking.

...behold, Satan has desired to have you,
> that he may sift you as wheat:
> But I have prayed for you,
> that your faith fails not:
> and when you are converted,
> strengthen your brethren.
> Luke 22:31-32(KJV)

This is the verse that resonated in my heart for decades. Being sifted like wheat shook my entire foundation. *"...the removing of those things that are shaken, as of things that are made, that those things which cannot be shaken may remain." Hebrews 12:27(KJV)* When my life feels unstable, I analyze those things that need released and find the things that are unshakeable and worthy of my investment.

Evaluate

How do you quiet the savage beast within you?

What things are out of balance in your life that you would like to change?

If you suffer with a life characterized by confusion and are willing to admit the problem and take a conscientious look at your dysfunctional thinking and behaviors, then this book is for you. Is it a quick fix? No, it is a journey of awareness to see the lies you believe and learn to observe your behaviors and acknowledge how your thinking is dangerously left of center.

Principles

1) Indulging exaggerated emotions produces chaos and torment.
2) Freedom from mental torment is work.
3) The armor of God is my responsibility to "put on".
4) Walking in the Fruit of the Spirit is my responsibility.
5) If I allow an offense in my life, my fruit will be lost.
6) Great peace belongs to those who learn to not give or take an offense.
7) Allowing an offense is bondage.
8) Wounds keep me bitter and emotionally immature.
9) I reap what I sow.
10) I can't rise higher than my emotions.
11) Forgiveness releases me from mental bondage.
12) Faithfulness in the little things develops faithfulness in the bigger things.

Tormented Mind Cycle
Lesson 1

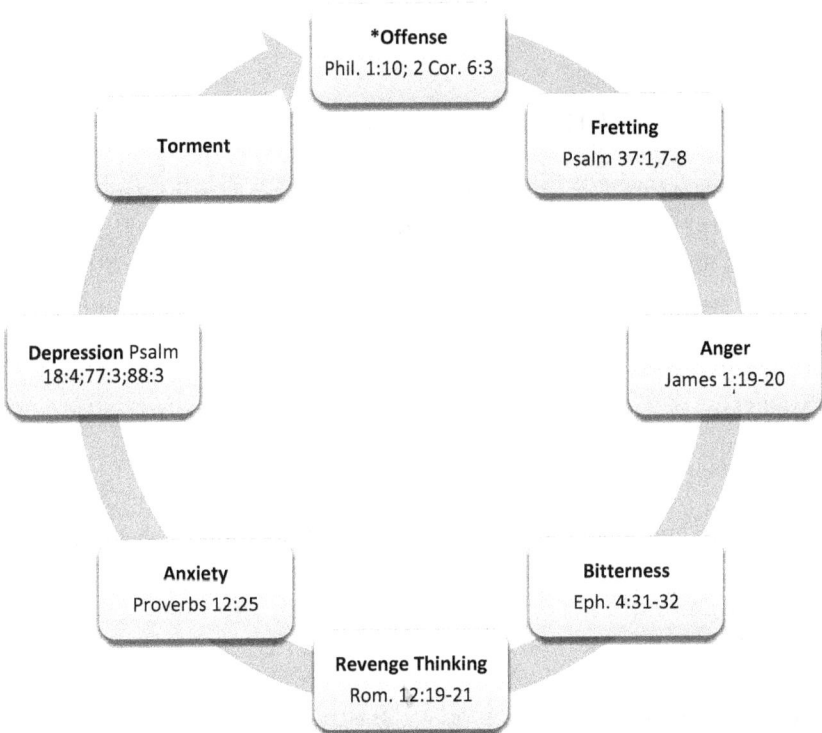

*Offense
Phil. 1:10; 2 Cor. 6:3

Fretting
Psalm 37:1,7-8

Torment

Anger
James 1:19-20

Depression Psalm 18:4;77:3;88:3

Bitterness
Eph. 4:31-32

Anxiety
Proverbs 12:25

Revenge Thinking
Rom. 12:19-21

There are three types of Mental Torment

	Tormented Spirit	
Inward	Subconscious	Outward
Self-destructive	Physical Problems	Raging/Abusive

Introduction

The person who exhibits **inward torment** develops exaggerated anxiety which ends in fear, anxiety or depression. This person may or may not have the ability to know when or where the torment started. They may not be able to trace the torment back to a particular event. Another form of **subconscious torment** can be identified by physical ailments: stomach problems, eating disorders, sleeplessness, physical sickness, twitching, choking while swallowing. There is a pervading looming anxiety over their entire life. This feels like a life characterized by tight rope walking.

The person who exhibits **outward torment** has exaggerated emotions. Exaggerated crying, moodiness, and racing thoughts. They often express their internal torment externally. There is a hyper focus on the temporal and trivial. Nothing seems to please them. Extreme levels of unleashed torment drive them to rage, abusing themselves or others. You often see cutting or other self-destructive behaviors with addictions or even suicidal thinking. The cutting or the addictive behaviors give them temporary relief from their extreme torment. These are destructive coping strategies.

Lesson
Learn to recognize when you are in a tormented mind cycle.

1) **Offense** Being offended skews our ability to discern what is best for our lives. Taking an offense, leaves us with motives that may be impure. It seems an offense sets us up to be a magnet for chaos. The chaos increases our confusion and everything good we are trying to accomplish seems to be misaligned with an evil force or at the very least produces an unfruitful life of nagging unease.

"...so that you may be able to discern what is best and may be pure and blameless (without offense) for the day of Christ." Philippians 1:10

"We put no stumbling block (offense) in anyone's path, so that our ministry will not be discredited (blamed)." 2 Corinthians 6:3

2) **Fretting** is a sister to murmuring, grumbling, and obsessive rumination. Recognizing fretting is half the battle. The next step will be to identify what person or circumstance (past or present) is driving the fretting and

empower our self to make a plan of recovery. Fretting takes energy and strength and potentially leaves us drained and helpless to make a healthy decision for our lives.

*"**Do not fret** because of those who are evil or be envious of those who do wrong... **Be still** before the LORD and **wait patiently** for him; **do not fret** when people succeed in their ways, when they carry out their wicked schemes. **Refrain from anger** and **turn from wrath**; **do not** fret—it only leads to evil." Psalms 37:1,7-8*

It's clear: **Do not fret!** The verses are acknowledging that people are doing evil, wrong, succeeding in wrongdoing and wicked schemes, but then it instructs us that if we fret, it will only lead to evil. The person in the wrong is wrong. But *our fretting makes us part of the problem.* So, what are we to do? Be still (quiet) and patient. If we recognize we our fretting and refuse to fret, we can use our strength to smile and enjoy the day. The torment is then unable to cling to us. This is counter intuitive and requires **emotional maturity**.

3) **Anger** If I am angry at someone, do I need to communicate it immediately? **Remember: Anger blames someone else. Instead, accept my portion of the responsibility.**

- *"My dear brothers and sisters, take note of this: Everyone should be quick to listen, slow to speak and slow to become angry, because human anger does not produce the righteousness that God desires." James 1:19-20*

Am I quick to listen? Am I slow to speak?

Wait before expressing anger:

During the waiting, you will analyze and claim your own part of the problem. If you do this wrong, the waiting will turn into a weapon of bitterness and you will build a case against someone else for the offense. But once you learn to rapidly release anger, this process can be done quicker. RULE: Do not speak until you have control over your emotions and can speak out of love and not anger. I usually wait three days, then:

  - o   I can't remember why I was angry.

- I realized it was a trauma memory and I was overreacting and very happy I didn't say anything.
- I have found a gentle way to discuss the situation with the person who needs corrected or coached.
- Or I decided the person isn't worth it and isn't approachable and would abuse me and I take it to the Lord and leave it.

4) **Bitterness** is an attitude that destroys present and future enjoyment of a relationship. Bitterness can be from abuse, neglect, unmet needs or simply unmet expectations. I know if I am bitter, because I can't let go of something that happened or something I expected to happen.

- *Get rid of all bitterness, rage, and anger, brawling and slander, along with every form of malice. Ephesians 4:31*

Recovery:

- *Be kind and compassionate to one another, forgiving each other, just as in Christ God forgave you. Ephesians 4:32*

5) **Revenge** If bitterness is indulged and exaggerated it can quickly turn to revenge.

- *"Do not take revenge, my dear friends, but leave room for God's wrath, for it is written: "It is mine to avenge; I will repay," says the Lord. Romans 12:19*

Recovery:

- *On the contrary: "If your enemy is hungry, feed him; if he is thirsty, give him something to drink. In doing this, you will heap burning coals on his head." Do not be overcome by evil but overcome evil with good. Romans 12:20-21*

6) **Anxiety** There is much to be said about the weight of anxiety. It can certainly overshadow any enjoyment of the day. Most anxiety can be resolved by staying in the present moment and trusting things to work themselves out. My anxiety is exacerbated by controlling people and circumstances. **There is freedom in allowing others to make mistakes and find their own path in life.**

"Anxiety weighs down the heart, but a <u>kind word</u> cheers it up." Proverbs 12:25

7) **Depression** The weight of chronic unresolved issues in our life can end in despair. There is a wrestling with our self that needs to be done. Many who sink into depression have an all good or bad mentality. The psalmist David took all his expressions of depression straight to the throne of God.

- *"The cords of death entangled me; the torrents of destruction overwhelmed me." Psalm 18:4*
- *"I remembered you, God, and I groaned; I meditated, and my spirit grew faint." Psalm 77:3*
- *"For my soul is full of trouble and my life draws near the grave." Psalm 88:3*

8) Torment **is extreme anxiety.**

Exercise
Evaluate the reasons why you may be stuck in torment.

Application
Recognize today how often your thinking is bound by an offense, fretting, anger, bitterness or anxiety and refuse this type of thinking.

Principle
Indulging exaggerated emotions produces chaos and torment.

Conclusion
A recognition of an offense that triggers this cycle is vital in recovery. A cognitive awareness of our behavioral patterns that follow is crucial. When we understand our cycle, then we can work through these behaviors and practice developing emotional maturity skills. The next two lessons are important in recovery. First, we will explore the mental replay loop that torment plays in our minds, explore lies we believe and build

mature thinking skills. Secondly, we will unravel all the thinking traps of torment.

The Lord is my rock, and my fortress, and my deliverer; my God, my strength, in whom I will trust; my buckler, and the horn of my salvation, and my high tower. Psalm 18:2

Lord, help us to recognize our torment and know that we can be delivered and live free from fretting, anxiety and depression. Help us to trust you with all the outcomes in our lives. Give us the power of emotional maturity, love and a sound mind. (2 Timothy 1:7 KJV) In Jesus Name, Amen

Mental Torment Evaluation

Evaluate your prison thinking. A=Always, N=Never, S=Sometimes.

Reasons We may be Stuck in Tormentors Prison Mark the ones you need to work through:	
1. Bad habit formed over the years; learned behavior or passed on from family	
2. Indulging Self-pity through undisciplined thinking	
3. Bringing up past (mounting up offenses)	
4. Focus on self and not Christ	
5. Fatigue, lack of sleep. Do I need to take care of myself, eat right, exercise and rest?	
6. Having recently talked to or been with an angry person. Proverbs 22:24-25	
7. Offenses from others; some people are not safe to confront. Proverbs 9:7-8	
8. Helpless feeling.	
9. Frustration with deeper unresolved issues or repetitive trauma.	
10. Money stress.	
11. Unchangeable circumstances – sickness, pain, etc.	
12. Stuck in grieving cycle.	
13. Refusing to forgive another, locks the prison door.	

Unwinding the Tormented Thinking
Lesson 2

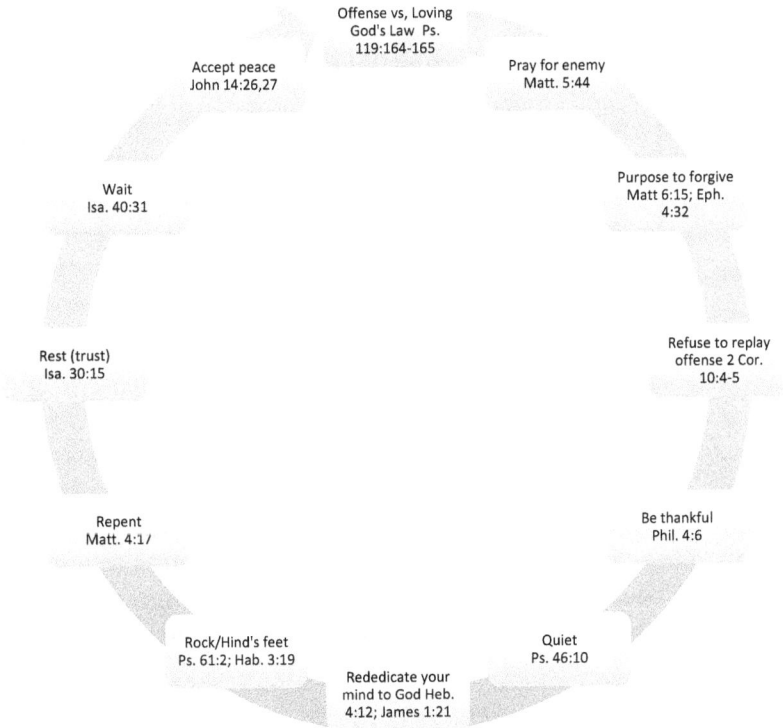

Offense vs, Loving God's Law Ps. 119:164-165

Accept peace John 14:26,27

Pray for enemy Matt. 5:44

Wait Isa. 40:31

Purpose to forgive Matt 6:15; Eph. 4:32

Rest (trust) Isa. 30:15

Refuse to replay offense 2 Cor. 10:4-5

Repent Matt. 4:17

Be thankful Phil. 4:6

Rock/Hind's feet Ps. 61:2; Hab. 3:19

Quiet Ps. 46:10

Rededicate your mind to God Heb. 4:12; James 1:21

Introduction

There is no reason for any of us to carry an offense. Until we recognize we are tormented, we will not know we are offended and have unraveling work to do. Let's discuss the spiritual life skills you need to become a mature believer in the wake of torment. There is a precept, principle, statute, commandment or life example to guide all our decisions in the Bible.

All Scripture is God-breathed and is useful for teaching, rebuking, correcting and training in righteousness, so that the servant of God may be thoroughly equipped for every good work.
2 Timothy 3:16

Lesson

1) **Offense** We are starting with the same offense in the Torment cycle. But this time, we will overcome the offense through the Word of God. *Seven times a day I praise you for your righteous laws. Great peace have those who love your law and nothing can make them stumble. Psalm 119:164-165*

2) **Pray for enemy** *But I tell you, love your enemies and pray for those who persecute you... Matthew 5:44*

3) **Purpose to forgive** *But if you do not forgive others their sins, your Father will not forgive your sins. Matthew 6:15; Be kind and compassionate to one another, forgiving each other, just as in Christ God forgave you. Ephesians 4:32*

4) **Refuse to replay offense** *The weapons we fight with are not the weapons of the world. On the contrary, they have divine power to demolish strongholds. We demolish arguments and every pretension that sets itself up against the knowledge of God, and we take captive every thought to make it obedient to Christ. 2 Corinthians 10:4-5*

5) **Be thankful** *...the Lord is near. Do not be anxious about anything, but in every situation, by prayer and petition, with thanksgiving, present your requests to God. Philippians 4:5b-6*

6) **Quiet** *... Be still and know that I am God. Psalm 46:10*

7) **Rededicate your mind to God** *It still remains for some to enter that rest, and since those who formerly had the good news proclaimed to them did not go in because of their disobedience.... Today if you hear his voice, do not harden your hearts. There remains, then a Sabbath-rest for the people of God; for anyone who enters God's rest also rests from their works, just as*

God did from his. Hebrews 4:6-7b; 9-10; **How?** *Therefore, get rid of all moral filth and the evil that is so prevalent and humbly(meekly) accept the word planted (engrafted) in you, which can save you. James 1:21.*

8) **Rock/Hind's feet** *...I call as my heart grows faint; lead me to the rock that is higher than I. Psalm 61:2; The Sovereign LORD is my strength; he makes my feet like the feet of a deer, he enables me to tread on the heights. Habakkuk 3:19*

9) **Repent** *"Repent, for the kingdom of heaven is at hand." Matthew 4:17(KJV)*

10) **Rest (trust)** *This is what the Sovereign LORD, the Holy One of Israel, says: "In repentance and rest is your salvation, in quietness and trust is your strength..." Isaiah 30:15*

11) **Wait** *But they that wait (hope) upon the LORD shall renew their strength; they shall mount up with wings as eagles; they shall run, and not be weary; and they shall walk, and not faint. Isaiah 40:31 (KJV)*

12) **Accept peace** *But the Counselor, the Holy Spirit, whom the Father will send in my name, will teach you all things and will remind you of everything I have said to you. Peace I leave with you; my peace I give you. I do not give to you as the world gives. Do not let your hearts be troubled and do not be afraid. John 14:26-27*

Exercise

If we are offended, we will STUMBLE! Recognize when you are offended and forgive quickly. You may become offended quicker if it is an old trauma wound that is being triggered. Go back and uncover the original offense and release the person or circumstance to God through following the unwinding the tormented thinking.

Application

The Fear of the Lord is foundational and releases hidden treasures for us to find.

"and if you look for it as for silver and search for it as for <u>hidden treasure</u>, then you will understand the fear of the LORD and find the knowledge of God." Proverbs 2:4-5

Spiritual Maturity Skills
Singing- Psalm 100:2 Worship the Lord with gladness: come before Him with joyful songs.
Joy-Psalm 16:11 You make known to me the path of life; you will fill me with joy in your presence, with eternal pleasures at your right hand.
Grace-*See to it that no one falls short of the grace of God and that no bitter root grows up to cause trouble and defile many. Hebrews 12:15*

Principle

Freedom from mental torment is work.

We have to train our mind and thinking to think right thoughts. Try it for a day. The harder it is to think right thoughts; the more desperately I need to learn the mental gymnastics of great thinking.

Conclusion

There are things we need to think through, but not until we have control over our emotions. The thoughts that particularly need reigned in are the obsessive, tormenting thoughts about circumstances or situations we cannot change or control.

The Lord is my rock, and my fortress, and my deliverer; my God, my strength, in whom I will trust; my buckler, and the horn of my salvation, and my high tower. Psalm 18:2

Lord, there is no way we can walk in the spirit without Your help. Help us live above our emotions without condemnation and obey Your Word. As we develop these skills, let the peace of God rule our hearts. (Romans 8:1; Philippians 4:7)

Optional:

Philippians Are my thoughts: true, honest, just, pure, lovely, of good report, with virtue and worthy of praise. (Philippians 4:8) Refuse evil and unproductive thinking!!!

Thought Test Scale

1) Is it true?	
2) Is it noble?	
3) Is it right?	
4) Is it pure?	
5) Is it lovely?	
6) Is it admirable?	
7) Is it excellent?	
8) Is it praiseworthy?	

Take every thought and scrutinize it through this test. Does it pass? If not, kick it out!

Optional

Mental Torment Scale	A	N	S
Rate your answers: Always, Never, or Sometimes			
1) Repeating offenses in my head (day and night)			
2) It's not my fault. (rationalizing and justifying)			
3) Wounded emotionally (fretting, crying, depression, anger, etc.)			
4) Why don't they like me? (man pleaser)			
5) They are always mean. (all or nothing words)			
6) Making accusations and excuses (he did, she did, they did)			
7) I should have said... (building a case to defend your bitterness and anger)			
8) I will never do such and such again. (vow making)			
9) Manipulated with other's emotions (bullying, threatening, nagging, pleading, and crying)			
10) Pleaser (needing the approval of others)			
11) Fear of man (Making decisions based upon being			

fearful of displeasing another)			
12) Playing the victim (Triangulating others to take an offense with you against another)			

Offended Cycle
Lesson 3

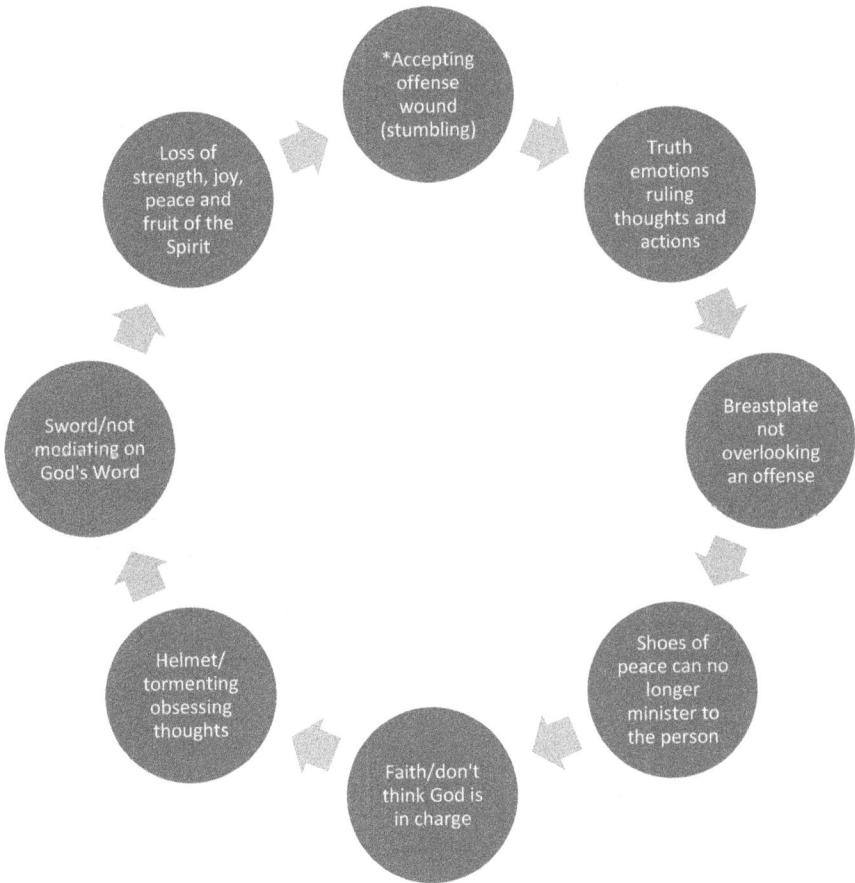

The cycle (clockwise from top):

- *Accepting offense wound (stumbling)
- Truth emotions ruling thoughts and actions
- Breastplate not overlooking an offense
- Shoes of peace can no longer minister to the person
- Faith/don't think God is in charge
- Helmet/ tormenting obsessing thoughts
- Sword/not meditating on God's Word
- Loss of strength, joy, peace and fruit of the Spirit

Introduction

Whenever we accept an offense, it begins to dismantle our armor.

Lesson

1) If you accept an offense, you will immediately begin to be defeated and stumble.
   Recognizing how you act, and what it feels like to take an offense is vitally important.
2) First, we lose the strong belt of truth and our emotions rule our thoughts and actions.
3) Then, we are no longer thinking, speaking or acting from our "Breastplate of Righteousness" instead we are acting from a worldly perspective. This can kick in selfishness, self-pity or your fight side that dominates or your flight side that runs and hides.
4) Next, you lost your shoes! Those carrying an offense are not walking in peace or able to minister to the one they are offended by and are ruled by emotions (anxiety, anger, bitterness, etc.)
5) Loss of Faith. You have forgotten God is in charge and He has a greater plan and you are to respond with gratefulness for what He is teaching you.
6) This is devastating. When your helmet is gone, your mind is tormented with obsessing/racing thoughts. This leads to depression and even suicide thinking.
7) You lost your weapon. You aren't remembering God's promises or meditating on Scripture. If you are reading the Word it is more difficult to understand, if you can understand it at all.
8) Your fruit is spoiled. There is a loss of strength, joy, peace and all the fruits of the Spirit.

Exercise

How has carrying an offense defeated me?

Application

If I indulge an offense, I have voluntarily given up my armor of protection. Identify your spiritual sickness.

Signs and Symptoms of Spiritual Sickness

- Despair (Eccles. 2:20)

- Fretful (Ps. 37:1,7 & 8)

- Fearful (Ps. 48:6)

- Double mindedness (James 4:8)

- Overwhelmed Spirit (Depression) (Ps. 55:5)

- Dismayed & Shame (Isa. 37:27)

- Depraved (reprobate) mind (Rom. 1:28)

- Quarrelsome (contentious) (Prov. 26:21)

- Darkened heart (vain imaginations) (Rom. 1:21)

- Pride (Prov. 13:10)

- Hopelessness (heart sick) (Prov. 13:12)

- Unbelief (Matt. 13:58)

- No rest (Heb. 4:6,10)

- Sad countenance (Neh. 2:2)

- Hardness of heart (Mark 16:14KJV)

Principle

The armor of God is our responsibility to "put on".
And that you put on the new man, which after God is created in righteousness and true holiness. Ephesians 4:24

Conclusion

The day of evil has come, and I am not dressed for battle!

The Lord is my rock, and my fortress, and my deliverer; my God, my strength in whom I will trust; my buckler, and the horn of my salvation, and my high tower. Psalm 18:2

Lord it is hard not to take an offense. We do it all the time without realizing it, let us become aware of when we take an offense. Show us how it makes us imbalanced and removes our armor. Let us be diligent to place firm but kind boundaries and never let anyone offend us again. Help us be the new man In Christ. In Jesus Name we pray.

Unraveling Offenses
Lesson 4

Armor of God

Truth

Fruit of the Spirit

Breastplate

Sword

Shoes of peace

Helmet of Salvation

Faith

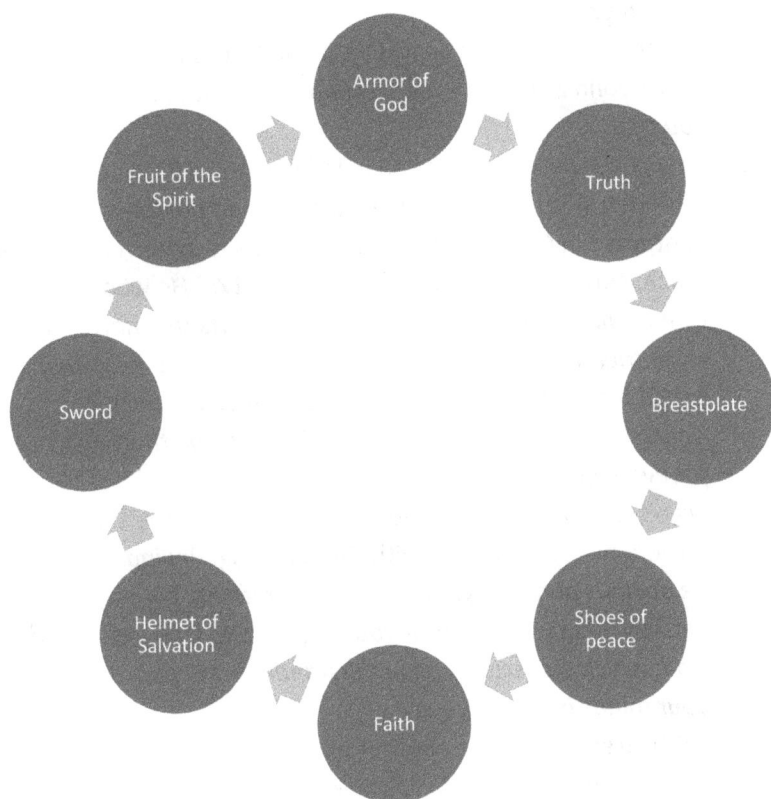

Introduction

Whenever we refuse an offense, we can enjoy the fruit of the Spirit.

Lesson

1) Put on the Whole Armor of God is developing maturity skills rooted in faith in God. *Romans 13:2 The night is nearly over; the day is almost here. So, let us put aside the deeds of darkness and put on the armor of light.*

2) The secret to letting the truth set you free is to "continue" in His Word. *John 8:32 Then you will know the truth and the truth will set you free.*

3) First cover the transgression in love by not repeating it with an offended spirit. Once, we have established ourselves in love and continued in God's Word we can spiritually discern if we should teach, correct or rebuke (in love). *Prov. 17:9 He who covers over an offense promotes love, but whoever repeats the matter separates close friends. 2 Timothy 3:16 All Scripture is God-breathed and is useful for teaching, rebuking, correcting and training in righteousness, so that the man of God may be thoroughly equipped for every good work.*

4) I can't have anxiety and the shoes of peace at the same time. Any anxiety needs to be met with thanksgiving. *Philippians 4:6,7 Do not be anxious about anything, but in everything, by prayer and petition, with thanksgiving, present your requests to God. And the peace of God, which transcends all understanding, will guard your hearts and your minds in Christ Jesus.*

5) Faith strengthens one another and exhorts others to continue in faith through tribulation so the kingdom of God can come into our hearts. (Ponder that thought!) *Acts 14:22 ...strengthening the disciples and encouraging them to remain true to the faith. "We must go through many hardships to enter the kingdom of God..."*

6) The helmet to combat anxiety is the "hope of salvation". *1 Thessalonians 5:8 But since we belong to the day, let us be self-controlled, putting on faith and love as a breastplate, and the hope of salvation as a helmet.* Being "sober" means to have self-control. Control over my thoughts, actions and words.

7) The sword is associated with trusting in God's Word and His faithful promises. The Word will help us cut to the root of the problem. *Hebrews 4:12 For the word of God is living and active. Sharper than any double-edged sword, it penetrates even to dividing soul and spirit, joints and marrow; it judges the thoughts and attitudes of the heart.*

8) Walking in the fruit of the Spirit is walking with the Holy Spirit. It is crucifying the flesh and our own will and desires. It is cooperating with Christ to allow Him to shape us and mold us into His image by intentionally putting on the new man. *Colossians 3:9-10 ...take off your old self... put on the new self, which is being renewed in knowledge in the image of its Creator.*

Exercise

What would it look like to never be offended?

Application

Consider the last thing that offended you and exchange your response to the Fruit of the Spirit.

Signs of Spiritual Health	
• Love	
• Joy	
• Peace	
• Patience (forbearance, long-suffering)	
• Kindness	
• Goodness	
• Faithfulness	
• Meekness (Gentleness)	
• Self-control	
How healthy are you?	

Principle

Walking in the Fruit of the Spirit is my responsibility.

But the fruit of the Spirit is love, joy, peace, forbearance (long-suffering), kindness (gentleness), goodness, faithfulness, meekness (gentleness), and self-control against such there is no law. Those who belong to Christ Jesus have crucified the flesh with its passions and desires. Since we live by the Spirit, let us keep in step with the Spirit. Galatians 5:22-25

Conclusion

When my flesh is crucified, this means I subject my own will and desires to the will of God. I go against my immature emotions and I stand on the solid Rock foundation of Jesus Christ. I refuse to get into a sinking boat in a storm and be doubleminded any longer. *(James 1:8)* Stop rolling over for the enemy and gear up! Prepare for battle!

The Lord is my rock, and my fortress, and my deliverer; my God, my strength in whom I will trust; my buckler, and the horn of my salvation, and my high tower. Psalm 18:2

Lord Jesus, we need you! Awaken our spirits out of slumber (Matthew 25:5). Help us to watch and pray and be vigilant to seek you (Mark 14:38). Place upon us the armor of God and when we have done all we can do, let us stand. Amen

Finally, my brethren, be strong in the Lord, and in the power of his might. Put on the whole armor of God, that you may be able to **stand** *against the schemes of the devil.*
For we wrestle not against flesh and blood, but against powers, against the rulers of darkness of this world, against spiritual wickedness in high places.
Wherefore take unto you the whole armor of God, that you may be able to withstand in the evil day, and having done all, to **stand.**
Stand *therefore, having your loins girt about with* truth, *and having on the breastplate of* righteousness. *And your feet shod with the preparation of the gospel of* peace.
Above all, taking the shield of faith, *wherewith you shall be able to quench all the fiery darts of the wicked.*

And take the helmet of <u>salvation</u>, and the sword of the Spirit, which is the <u>Word of God</u>.

<u>Praying</u> always with all <u>prayer and supplication</u> in the Spirit and <u>watching</u> thereunto with all <u>perseverance</u> and <u>supplication</u> for all saints.

And for me, that utterance may be given unto me, that I may <u>open my mouth boldly</u>, to make known the mystery of the gospel. For which I am an ambassador in bonds: that therein I may <u>speak boldly</u>, as I ought to speak. Ephesians 6:10-20KJV

Offense aka an Emotional Wound
Lesson 5

Introduction

Offense: resentment, to wound the feelings of another, to displease or anger, do wrong or transgress. This Greek word (KJV Strong's Concordance) suggest if we are offended that it will entrap us, trip us, entice us to sin, make us stumble or fall into apostasy. *Apostasy* means to refuse to follow, obey or recognize a religious faith (Merriam-Webster).

Without Offense: Faultless, inoffensive, irreproachable, unblemished (Merriam-Webster).

Lesson

Mark 4:4-9; 14-20
Way Side—This person's heart is hardened by sin (not penetrable by the Word). He is open to Satan.
Stony Ground—This person's heart is prideful, thick and calloused. It is quickly and easily offended.
Thorny Ground—This person's heart is dull. He has lots of idols, his eyes are on temporal things. He is fretful, anxious, not in the Word and easily distracted.
Good Ground—This person has good character. His heart is soft and plowed, fertile and ready to hear the Word and receive the seed and grow. He has been well trained in the knowledge of morals, ethics, standards, laws, truth and obedience. He studies the precepts, principles, statutes and commandments of God's Words to guide his life's decisions.

WAY SIDE	STONY GROUND
• Satan comes to steal the Word immediately and takes what was sown in their heart. (Lost)	• Receives with gladness • No root/endure for a time • Affliction/Persecution

	comes *offended* (Lost? Backslidden)

SOWN AMONG THORNS
• Hears Word
• Word is choked
    ○ By the cares of the world
    ○ Deceitfulness of riches
    ○ Lust of things
    ○ ***Offended***
Unfruitful (Saved but fruit lost!)
	GOOD GROUND
	• Hears Word and receives it
	• Good character
	• Much Fruit!!!
	• Produces fruit 30, 60, 100-fold
	• Very fruitful. Growing and disciplining others!
	Saved and fruitful

Exercise

Read Mark 4:23-25 (23) *"If anyone has ears to hear, let him hear."* (24) *"Consider carefully what you hear,"* he continued. *"With the measure you use, it will be measured to you and even more. (25) Whoever has will be given more; whoever does not have even what he has will be taken from him."* (See answers below)

1) Verse 24 find the secret to receiving more truth.
2) Verse 25 What happens if we don't receive the truth?
3) Verse 23 How do we know we are talking about truth and not wheat or some other kind of material thing?

Answers:
1) Receive the Word we have heard. 2) The truth we have gets taken away from us.
3) He that has an ear let him hear.

Application

Yield any offense to God immediately through the use of flare prayers and ask for an opportunity to minister to the one who is offending you. We have no peace when we carry an offense and will not be able to focus fully on the Lord. *Matthew 5:9 Blessed are the peacemakers...* If we carry an offense for an extended period of time, it will become a wound. A wound becomes bitterness and bitterness defiles and robs us of the grace of God *(Hebrews 12:15)*. Any correction needs to be done in love so there is no guilt, shame or condemnation. *(Galatians 6:1)*

Principle

If you allow an offense in your life, your fruit will be lost.

Conclusion

Emotional immaturity tends to mirror the emotion that is in front of them. Learn to "OWN" your own emotions and not bounce off of other people's emotions. *(Proverbs 25:28; 16:32)* Learn to allow others to vent and own their own emotions. Learn to detach emotionally from offenses.

Real beauty is that quiet and gentle spirit *(I Peter 3:4-5)*. The secret to controlling our emotions is to have transformed thinking through the mind of Christ. *(Romans 12:1-2: 1 Corinthians 2:16)*. Think before you speak *(James 1:26)*.

The Lord is my rock, and my fortress, and my deliverer; my God, my strength, in whom I will trust; my buckler, and the horn of my salvation, and my high tower. Psalm 18:2

O Precious Savior, Jesus, Our Lord, thank you for giving us your Word and instructions on how not to take an offense. Lord steady our feet and keep us from stumbling. Let us never be a stumbling block for another. Give us a soft and tender heart to forgive quickly and repent quickly. In Jesus Name we pray, Amen.

Optional

How to Stop an Offense	
1) Is this about me?	
2) Are they reacting to my sin?	
3) Is God teaching me something in this situation?	
4) Is this person stressed and needs comforted?	

5) Is this person dealing with overwhelming losses and need to grieve?	
5) Is it an old trauma wound being triggered, and needs healed and released to God?	
6) Is this person feeling physically ill or dealing with chronic pain?	
7) Is this person overreacting because of something I have done to them in the past that isn't resolved?	

Types of Offenses	
1) We need the Word of God, so we know what is coming and we won't be offended by the world and persecution. John 16:1	**No offense**
2) When persecution comes, many will be offended and betray and hate each other. Matthew 24:10	**Unrighteous Offense**
3) If we savor the things of men, we will be a stumbling block to others. Matthew 16:23	**Offense to God**
4) Jesus was righteously offended because the people were being cheated and He corrected the situation. Matthew 21:12-13	**Righteous Offense**

How to Be Blameless
Lesson 6

Introduction

A blameless person is pleasant and does not take an offense or engage others with exaggerated emotions. They are surrounded by many people who adore them and are eager to please them. So, understanding how to recognize an offense and release it quickly is key to not developing a wound and ending up in a trauma cycle with insecure attachments and constantly dealing with exaggerated emotional triggers. These exaggerated emotions turn into tormenting anxiety. Today, we are going to work on some skills of communication and boundary setting. This skill of being blameless (not offended) must be practiced intentionally.

Lesson

1) A mature believer will refuse to take an offense. *Psalms 119:165 Great peace have they who love your law, and nothing can make them stumble (offended).* <u>Secret </u> to not taking an offense is in *Psalm 119:164. Seven times a day will I praise You, for your righteous laws.*

2) Show deference (amicable, congenial, cordial, friendly, sociable) and attempt to not offend a friend. *Proverbs 18:19 (KJV) A brother offended is harder to be won than a strong city...*

3) When we cause an offense or a scandal the ministry is discredited. *2 Corinthians 6:3 We put no stumbling block (offense) in anyone's path, so that our ministry will not be discredited.*

4) When we abound in knowledge and depth of insight, we can be pure and blameless (without offense). *Philippians 1:9-10 And this is my prayer: that your love may abound more and more in knowledge and depth of insight, so that you may be able to discern what is best and may be pure and blameless (without offense) until the day of Christ.*

5) Do ALL THINGS without complaining or arguing. *Philippians 2:14-15 Do everything without complaining or arguing, so that you may become blameless (without offense) and pure, children of God without fault in a crooked and depraved generation, in which you shine like stars in the universe.*

6) Stop judging others and don't be a stumbling block or obstacle to your friend. *Romans 14:13 Therefore let us stop passing judgment on one another. Instead, make up your mind not to put any stumbling block or obstacle in your brother's way.*

7) Set a boundary and avoid those who are divisive or offensive. *Romans 16:17 I urge you, brothers, to watch out for those who cause divisions and put obstacles in your way that are contrary to the teaching you have learned.*

Exercise

Discuss practical applications to show deference and not take an offense.

Application

Living in a crooked and perverse generation describes the general atmosphere of our current culture. When we can rise above our emotions and live by the principles of God's Word, there is great reward. The reward of a home full of peace and without strife is priceless. Set your goal today to recognize offenses, clear them up quickly and show deference or friendliness by not taking an offense. This does not mean you are a doormat. No, not at all. Instead, we will use boundaries and establish distance between us and divisive behaviors. If this isn't possible, then we can learn to detach and distance our hearts emotionally. Whenever I correct a child, I do this with gentleness but firmness. Then I return to make sure the child knows I love them and am not offended with them. Then, we can have a fresh start.

Principle

Great peace belongs to those who learn to not give or take an offense.

Conclusion

Learning to not take an offense takes humility. Ask God for help. Avoid those who love to argue. *Proverbs 29:9 (KJV) If a wise man contends with a foolish man, whether he rage or laugh, there is no rest.* Complaining and grumbling is contagious. Walk away from it.

If you are in an abusive situation, I expect you to stand up for yourself and find legal counsel, legal help and a safe shelter to escape. You need to take enough of an offense to empower yourself to stand up for you and your children. Instead of being offended, use your energy to develop a plan of escape. There is no excuse for physical, verbal, financial, emotional, spiritual, or sexual domination or abuse. There just isn't.

The Lord is my rock, and my fortress, and my deliverer; my God, my strength in whom I will trust; my buckler, and the horn of my salvation, and my high tower. Psalm 18:2

Dear God, in the name of Jesus Christ our Savior, we pray you would help us to not take an offense or be an offense or a stumbling block to anyone else. Lord, give us your gentle teaching and help us to remember to practice the skill of "not taking or giving an offense" in the workplace, at church or in our homes. Help us to break bad habits of complaining and arguing. We will give You all the praise, the honor and glory. Amen.

Who Needs a Boundary?
• Those who complain and argue. *(Philippians 2:14)*
• Those who are divisive and easily offended. *(Romans 16:17)*
• Those who use fair speech to deceive the simple. *(Romans 16:18)*

• Recognize the divisive by identifying those who:
     o Have confusion around their life.
     o Are opinionated and setting up sides.
     o Are gossiping behind another's back.
     o Serve themselves.

Reasons to Avoid Offense
Philippians 2:14-16
1) We will be blameless and harmless.
2) We will be Sons of God.
3) We will be without rebuke.
4) We will be shining lights in a dark world.
5) We will hold forth the Word of Life.
6) We will rejoice in the day of Christ.
7) Our labor won't be in vain.

Yoke of Slavery
Lesson 7

Introduction

Do not coddle a tormented demeanor. A tormented mind can be turned inward and develop into destructive thinking. This could produce fretting, and chronic ruminating on unsolvable problems. It could lead to depression, addiction or suicidal thinking. Internal torment, also, yields chronic physical ailments. External torment manifest as bullying, raging or verbal abuse. When it's on a slow brew you will see murmuring, grumbling and irritability. There is a deliverance and a freedom. Refuse this yoke of slavery. *It is for freedom that Christ has set us free. Stand firm, then, and do not let yourselves be burdened again by a yoke of slavery. Galatians 5:1*

Lesson
Reasons to Not Take an Offense

1) Anger will never produce righteousness. *James 1:20 ...for man's anger does not bring about the righteous life that God desires.*
2) Two wrongs don't make a right. *James 2:20 You foolish man, do you want evidence that faith without deeds (works) is useless?*
3) It is developing character. *Hebrews 13:21 ...equip you with everything good for doing his will, and may he work in us what is pleasing to him...*
4) God has a plan we cannot see. Jeremiah 29:11-13 "For I know the plans I have for you," declares the Lord, "plans to prosper you and not to harm you, plans to give you hope and a future."
5) It is living in the past and not reaching for the future. *Philippians 3:13 ...one thing I do: forgetting what is behind and straining towards what is ahead.*
6) It will make us weary or faint. *Hebrews 12:3 Consider him who endured such opposition from sinful men, so that you will not grow weary and lose heart.*
7) We will lose our joy. *James 1:2 Consider it pure joy, my brothers, whenever you face trials of many kinds.*

8) It is forgetting to trust the Lord. *Proverbs 3:5 Trust in the Lord with all your heart and lean not on your own understanding.*
9) It is a lack of understanding that all things can work for good. *Romans 8:28 And we know that in all things God works for the good of those who love him, who have been called according to his purpose.*

Exercise
Choose a reason to not take an offense and discuss it.

Application
Learning not to take an offense is a life maturity skill. Once I was with a very grumpy person who desperately needed my help. I consistently was offended and chronically tormented and did not want to help them. When I decided to just love them and not to take an offense, I cared for their needs and understood their emotional pain and developed a heart of compassion for them. The mental torment stopped, and I could enjoy the good part of the relationship and set boundaries with their emotional immaturity.

Principle
Allowing an offense is bondage.

Conclusion
When we are not offended, we will start to grow and be transformed. We can begin to develop the fruit of the Spirit. Our countenances will radiate with newness of life. Not taking an offense is more than thinking positive thoughts. It is a renewed mind that thinks God's thoughts. It is living with an eternal perspective and not with a temporal view. If you are still in the stench of the graveclothes of offense, connect with strong believers and let them obey the command of Christ at the resurrection of Lazarus to "Loose him and let him go." *(John 11:43-44KJV)* Offenses bind us to the temporal. God wants our eyes fixed on the eternal.

The Lord is my rock, and my fortress, and my deliverer; my God, my strength in whom I will trust; my buckler, and the horn of my salvation, and my high tower. Psalm 18:2

Lord Jesus, our beloved Savior, thank you for these lessons of maturity. Shape us and mold us into your image that we may be more like you. Let us live under your presence that nothing or no one has the power to offend us ever again. In Jesus name, Amen.

Optional

A Yoke of Slavery	
• Offended easily	
• Carries emotional wounds	
• Anxiety	
• Increased stress	
• Exaggerated emotions	
• Increased trauma	
• Double-minded	
• Unstable in all your ways	
• Indecisive	
• Contentious/arguing	
• Lack of connectedness	
• Bitter and more bitter	
• Overwhelmed/Depression	
• Rehearsing regrets	

Wounded Heart
Lesson 8

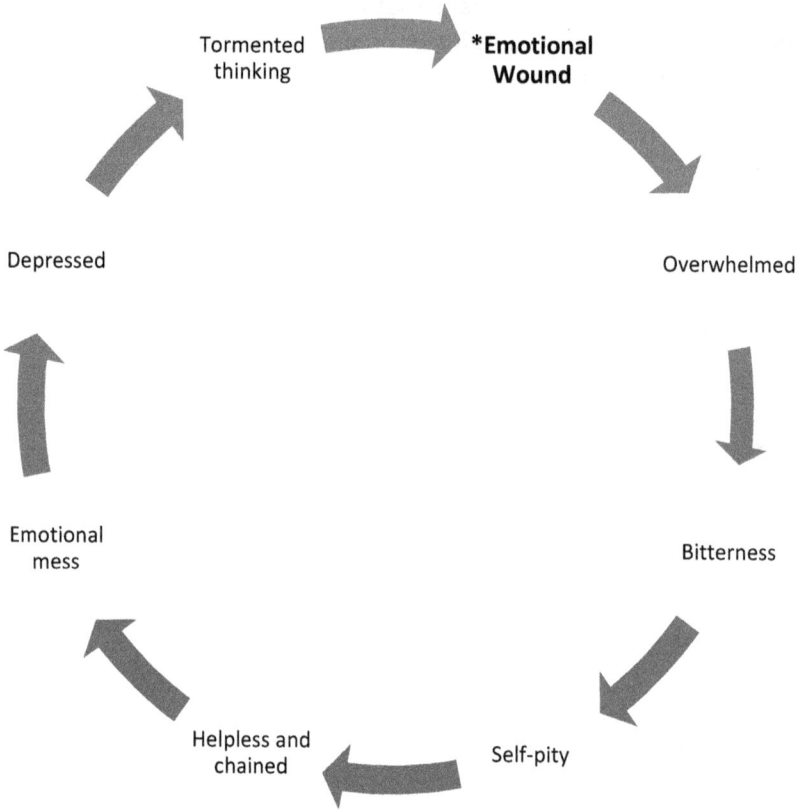

Tormented thinking → *Emotional Wound

*Emotional Wound → Overwhelmed

Overwhelmed → Bitterness

Bitterness → Self-pity

Self-pity → Helpless and chained

Helpless and chained → Emotional mess

Emotional mess → Depressed

Depressed → Tormented thinking

Introduction

First, we are going to evaluate what caused our wounds. Next, we will analyze each developing stage of a festering wound. We will identify how to change from being emotionally ruled and explore how to take control of our lives by detaching from people and emotions that are not safe.

Recovering ourselves from a wounded heart, is a simple shift in our thinking. It is not easy, but simple. Discovering our wounds and facing them can feel like a turbulent sea, you may need a support person to explore this with you. Do not give up! Our recovery from a wounded heart comes next!

Lesson
Identifying your Wounded Heart

1) **Unresolved Emotional Wounds** - Until we **identify the wound (or the guilt) that drives the self-destructive patterns of thinking and behaviors**, it is going to be difficult to find lasting peace. *A man's spirit sustains him in sickness, but a crushed (wounded) spirit who can bear? Proverbs 18:14*

Wound Identifier
• List all my wounds (guilt). Are they in the past, current or ongoing?
• List unsafe people and environments. Are they in the past, current or ongoing?
• Which people need firm boundaries?
• Which people do I need to avoid altogether?
• List the semi-safe people who you can visit for short periods of time after emotionally detaching from them.
• List the people who make you crazy and need to be avoided.

I love lists. They help me see black and white. When I can identify my crazy makers by their past behaviors and lies. I can set up boundaries. Then, I am not sucked into the game again. If you do not feel free to write, journal this dialogue in your head so you can visualize what is going on in your life by stepping back from the emotions and chaos and discover the facts.

2) **Overwhelmed - A thought or feeling that overpowers me with grief, fear, guilt, or shame. This causes us not to trust our self.** *The chords of death entangled me; the torrents of destruction (floods of ungodly men) overwhelmed me (made me afraid). Psalm 18:4*

Overwhelmed
• What emotion is overwhelming?
• What thoughts or circumstances are fearful?
• What causes my anxiety?
• What makes me angry?
• Was there one traumatic event that began my imbalance and made me feel overwhelmed?

Emotional Responses to A Wound
• Do I stay in bed?
• Do I get moody and withdrawn?
• Do I start fantasy thinking/daydreaming attempting to escape reality?
• What does my self-talk say when circumstances are beyond my control?
• Does my thinking become obsessive?
• Does this trigger my Substance Use Disorder?

If we can identify the destructive thinking, we can interrupt the behaviors that follow by changing our thinking.

3) **Bitterness - marked by intensity and severity of physical and emotional suffering.** *For I see that you are full of bitterness and captive to sin. Acts 8:23* **The one with abusive behaviors is not usually safe to**

confront. Then my stomach churns and I develop restlessness and I cannot sleep soundly. **Unnecessary harshness from me causes more bitter responses from others.** We must learn to process this bitterness and push it outside of us and not identify with it or it will eat us up from the inside out.

Bitterness Evaluation
What kind of bitterness is in my life? (Example: Domestic violence, controlling spouse, parents, or boss, those with smooth talking deception, irritating co-worker, emotionally unavailable mate, etc.)
What kind of behaviors do I do that increases bitter circumstances in my life? (Example: Manipulation, stubbornness, cursing, defiance against authority, frequent conflicts, complaining, arguing, lying, manipulating, gossiping, slandering, brooding, or acting moody.)

3) **Self-pity - a self-indulgent musing on my own misfortunes, suffering, and sorrows.** *"I loathe my very life; therefore. I will give free rein to my complaint (upon myself) and speak out in the bitterness of my soul." Job 10:1* When I first started identifying my self-pity, I was shocked at how much of it I indulged. The focus in my life was on the empty or destructive relationships and my resulting unmet needs. This would position me in a tailspin and bring up a legion of past wounds I had not resolved. This was a self-comforting behavior. Compassion or affirmation was greatly lacking from others in my life. So, **brooding, and self- pity had become my dysfunctional friends.** This response to my circumstances made me stagnant and perpetually immature.

Just for the fun of it, take one day and count the times you indulge self-pity, sulking, pouting, whining, and withdrawing.

4) **Helpless and chained - defenseless and without support.** *If trouble comes upon them, ... they are enslaved and afflicted...Job 36:8 (NLT)*

Recognition of this stage is easy. It can be characterized by isolation, curled up in my bed, paralyzed to trust others, binging on comfort food, television, shopping, calling off work, sexual fantasies, substance use, etc. These behaviors tend to slow the racing thoughts of anxiety and helplessness. Our racing thoughts can spiral on a negative loop and keep us anxious. Others may have no cognitive thoughts, only primal exaggerated emotions with an intense anger, grumpiness, or brooding. **What things or circumstances make you feel helpless?**

5) **Emotional Mess – No peace in my life.** *"Woe to me! The LORD has added sorrow to my pain; I am worn out with groaning and find no rest." Jeremiah 45:3* In this stage of carrying my wound alone, I go through the motions but enjoy nothing. **What problem is your peace hiding behind?**

6) **Depression – A time marked by sadness.** *All the days of the oppressed are wretched... Proverbs 15:15* This is the place where we realize this vicious cycle of depravity will never end for us, we feel stuck. This phase feels like death. There is great sadness.

Characteristic of Depression	
• Problems sleeping	
• Loss of appetite	
• Isolation	
• Crying	
• Anxiety	
• Memory loss/poor concentration	
• Racing thoughts	
• Emotionally numb	

7) Tormented – Obsessing and loss of identity. *See, O LORD, how distressed I am! I am in torment within, and in my heart, I am disturbed...there is only death. Lamentations 1:20* Obsessing and completely losing our identity, if not corrected, can lead to chronic stress and chronic health issues. It can also lead to mental breakdown and suicidal thinking, taking excessive prescription medications, or substance use disorder in an attempt to cope.

Exercise

Identify what kinds of things/circumstances make you feel bitter? This is easy to do. Listen to your complaints. Whatever you are grumbling about is what has made you bitter.

Principle

Wounds keep me bitter and emotionally immature.

Application

It is when we take control over our lives and say, "no more" that the healing can begin. First, I must admit there is an imbalance and a need to heal. This step brings to light the wound(s) which hold me back. In this phase, it is helpful to develop an internal dialogue. During these reflective moments, I am free to journal and feel all my feelings and thoughts.

Conclusion

Processing my thoughts through reflective thinking develops the realization that these emotions may be intensely exaggerated. If the abuse is active or if the one abusing me flips behaviors and pretends to be safe, I need the facts to empower me to protest by exercising my "No" muscle and distancing myself from the abuse.

When I know the facts, it breaks the confusion and its emotional control over me. Facts give me **mental thinking direction** which can separate me from my cycle of chaos and negativity and help me **reclaim my own identity**. It can give me permission to take control of my thoughts. Otherwise, people and circumstances dictate what I think and feel. That needs to stop! **Next, week we will unravel this mess!**

The Lord is my rock, and my fortress, and my deliverer; my God, my strength in whom I will trust; my buckler, and the horn of my salvation, and my high tower. Psalm 18:2

Father, In the name of Jesus, please help us recognize and release our bitterness so our wounds can heal. Give us a safe place internally to develop a relationship with You. Help us develop boundaries with those who abuse us and develop an identity in Christ so we may know we are "children of the living God" (Romans 9:26; Galatians 3:26; Philippians 2:15; 1 John 3:1-2).

Rest → *Emotional Wound → Reframe thinking → Intentionally forgive → Think good thoughts → Have compassion on enemies → Stay in the present → Seek Recovery → Rest

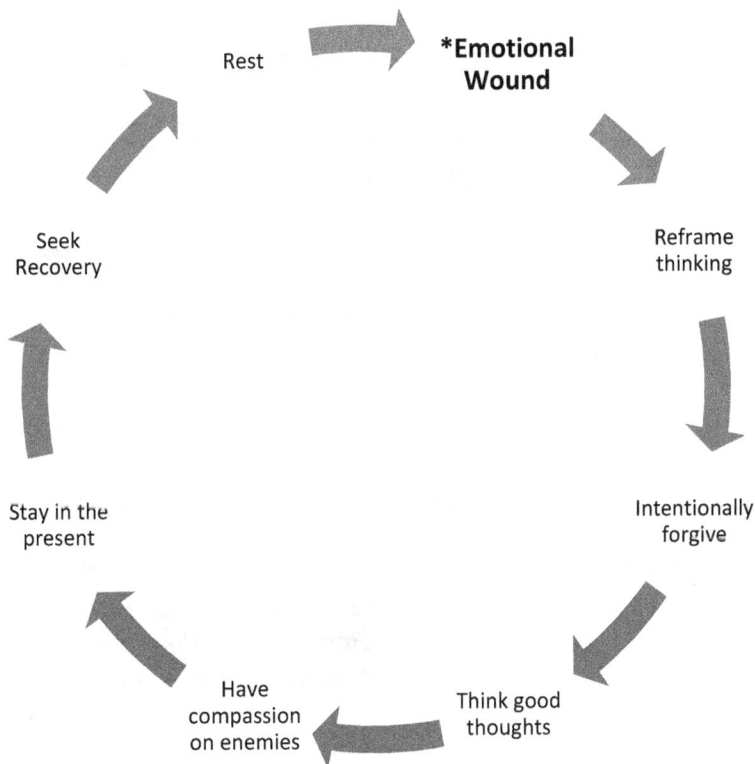

Introduction

It is vital to recognize our wounds and seek restorative healing. The goal is acceptance and peace. Then, we can use our energy to remove ourselves from the people and places that keep us in chaos. Wounds cause exaggerated emotions and foolish emotions, if indulged, take over our lives. Learning to not indulge destructive negative thinking is a skill that must be cultivated. We must have the truth of right thinking to direct our path. In this lesson, we will discuss some ways to heal from our wounds and set our feet firmly on solid ground. **Without sober emotions, relapse is dangerously close. Be patient with yourself. It takes time to conquer poor habits.**

Lesson

Do not take a wound inside of yourself, but instead use it as a springboard for growth.

1) **Emotional Wound** – Vulnerable to be wounded by people or circumstances.
So, I advise you to live according to your new life in the Holy Spirit. Then you will not be doing what your sinful nature craves. Galatians 5:16 (NLT) My weak nature has a meltdown with a wound and I indulge anxiety and fear and end up in confusion. This is the same wound as in the Wounded Heart Cycle, but today, we will take back our identity and respond in the Spirit and not with the flesh. **What would your life look like if you rejected this wound as if it never happened?**

2) **Reframe your thinking with truth.** Name your suffering. State the facts. *I consider that our present sufferings are not worth comparing with the glory that will be revealed in us. Romans 8:18* **What is the truth? Who is or was your offender? Is there anything you could have done differently to stop or correct the situation?**

3) **Purpose to forgive.** Forgiveness is an act of your will, not your emotions.
For if you forgive men when they sin against you, your heavenly Father will also forgive you. But if you do not forgive men their sins, your Father will not forgive your sins. Matthew 6:14-15 Forgiveness does not mean trusting this person again. Nor does it mean making myself available to be abused. It is a conscience and repeated choice to forgive every time I sense bitterness. I do this out of obedience, not because I feel like it. Eventually, my emotions follow, and I will have no animosity from the past abusive situation. Forgiveness sets me free.

4) **Think good thoughts.** Declare war on negative, self-defeating

48

thoughts!

The weapons we fight with are not the weapons of the world. On the contrary, they have divine power to demolish (pull down) strongholds. We demolish arguments (cast down imagination) and every pretension (high thing) that sets itself up against the knowledge of God, and we take captive every thought to make it obedient to Christ. 2 Corinthians 10:4-6

This takes purposeful planning. I change my self-talk. This lets me see myself differently and empowers me to change. Now tell your mountain of depression to move!

Turning it Over

Name negative things you say to yourself.	Now change the words.
I can't do anything right.	I can do whatever needs done and if I fail, I can try again.
I mess up everything.	I can be patient with myself.
You will never amount to anything.	I can make a plan and be kind to myself and learn from failure.
I am unlovable.	I can learn to love myself.
I have been told I not even worth the value of the food I eat.	I am infinitely valuable in Christ Jesus.
Ruminating and stressing over the past.	I can stay in the present to enjoy every moment.

Boundaries with those who are Abusive or Unsafe
1) I can be patient, kind and very firm.
2) I can distance myself.
3) I can hide myself.
4) I can be quiet and refuse to escalate the problem.
5) I can walk away.

5) **Have compassion on your enemies.** This breaks their tormenting power over your thought life. *But I say unto you, love your enemies, bless*

49

them that curse you, do good to them that hate you, and pray for them which despitefully use and persecute you. Matthew 5:44 (KJV)
This is something I do whether I feel like it or not. This is for me, not for them.

Keep a short list of offenses done to you and offenses you have done. Review the list every evening and ask forgiveness or forgive. I can do this with another person or on my own. This can be done through journaling. It is a simple act which can free me from carrying the burdens of the day. If the burden comes up again, I can remind myself to let it go again. Tomorrow, I can start with a clean slate!

6) **Stay in the present.** How do I do this? *Therefore, do not worry about tomorrow, for tomorrow will worry about itself. Each day has enough trouble of its own. Matthew 6:34*
I refuse worry, fretting or anxiety, and I place my full attention on whatever task is at hand. **Just because nonsense entered my head does not mean I have to entertain it**. I can use my willpower to kick it out and replace it with something worthwhile. Listening to pleasant music while I do dishes or clean is refreshing. Learning something new can stop the negative ruminating.

7) **Seek your recovery (deliverance).** *(4) I sought the LORD, and he answered me; he delivered me from all my fears. (7) The angel of the LORD encamps around those who fear him, and he delivers them. (17) The righteous cry out, and the LORD hears them; he delivers them from all their troubles. Psalm 34:4,7,17*

8) **Rest** *For anyone who enters God's rest also rests (ceases) from his own work, just as God did from his. Hebrews 4:10* If you aren't resting, you are doing your own work.

Exercise
Think of a past wound that has hindered your growth and work it through these 8 steps.

Principle
I reap what I sow.
I receive whatever I give!!! It is the principle of **sowing and reaping**. If I plant corn, I will not grow green beans. *Do not be deceived: God cannot be*

mocked. A man reaps what he sows. Galatians 6:7 They sow to the wind and reap the whirlwind. Hosea 8:7 **Negativity manifests itself in my life as anxiety and fear.**

One kernel can produce a hundred kernels of corn. Could one negative action, deed or thought reap a hundred like it? Likewise, could one kind and hopeful thought or response reap a hundred more positive interactions?

Application

Reframe the Wound
1) Evaluate your part in the problem. (You can only be responsible for yourself, not other adults.) Children who were molested have no responsibility for what happened. NONE!
2) Educate yourself on your responsibility to not make allowances for immature, irresponsible, or abusive adults.
3) Seek deliverance from the person(s) abusing or taking advantage of you. Set firm boundaries. Empower yourself.
4) Find safe people and places to build community, support groups and/or professional counseling.
5) Develop other interests: gardening, woodworking, crafting, photography, music, art... Find ways to invest in yourself.
6) **Relax (Rest).** Take a deep breath and let go of everything you can't fix.
7) **Pray deliverance** Scriptures from the Psalms.

Conclusion

There are some problems or repetitive thoughts that go on for decades. It is like going around and around the same block just with different scenarios. The conclusion is the same: I am helpless to change the situation. This could be an injustice in the present or past you cannot reconcile. It could be a circumstance outside of your control or a circumstance set up to control you. We can think of these things all day and night, but **there is no way to solve the unsolvable.** We cannot think our way through some problems or around it or past it and more rumination of the situation just **robs us of today.**

The Lord is my rock, and my fortress, and my deliverer; my God, my strength in whom I will trust; my buckler, and the horn of my salvation, and my high tower. Psalm 18:2

Father God help me to recognize my wounds and take them to the altar and release them to You. I forgive everyone who has hurt me. I give up my right to hold a grudge. Help me enjoy each day one moment at a time. In Jesus name I pray, Amen.

Drunk vs. Sober Emotions
Lesson 10

Introduction

Without sober emotions relapse is dangerously close. I find many in recovery for several years are still drunk with emotions. Drinking deeply of negative emotions ingrains us into a trauma cycle. Here is the cycle I observe:

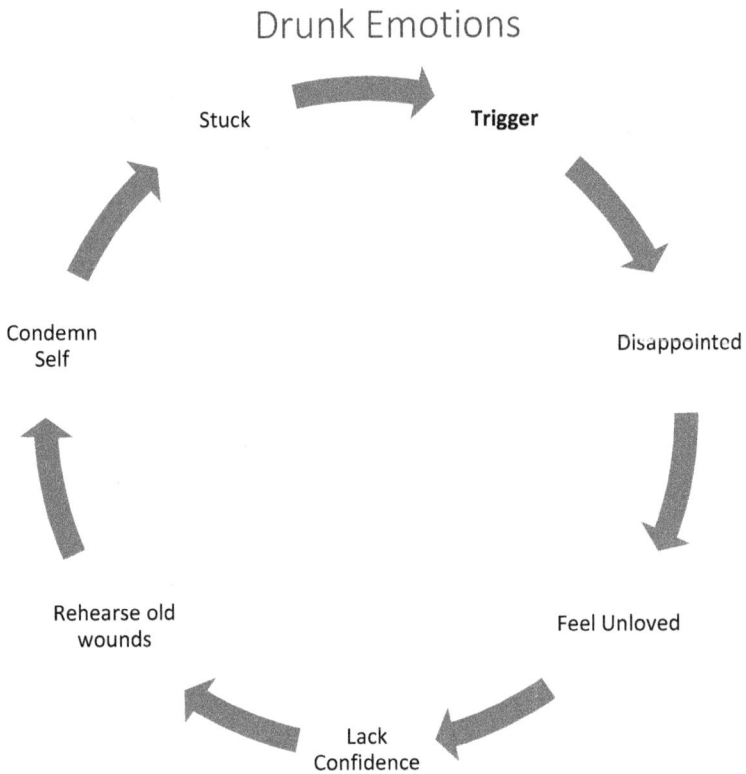

Drunk Emotions

Stuck → Trigger → Disappointed → Feel Unloved → Lack Confidence → Rehearse old wounds → Condemn Self → Stuck

Relapsed emotionally this morning? So what? Shake it off. Whether it is a chemical relapse into substance use or an emotional relapse into repetitive ingrained subconscious immature emotions, shake it off. There is no excuse to allow emotions to become dominant.

Sober Emotions

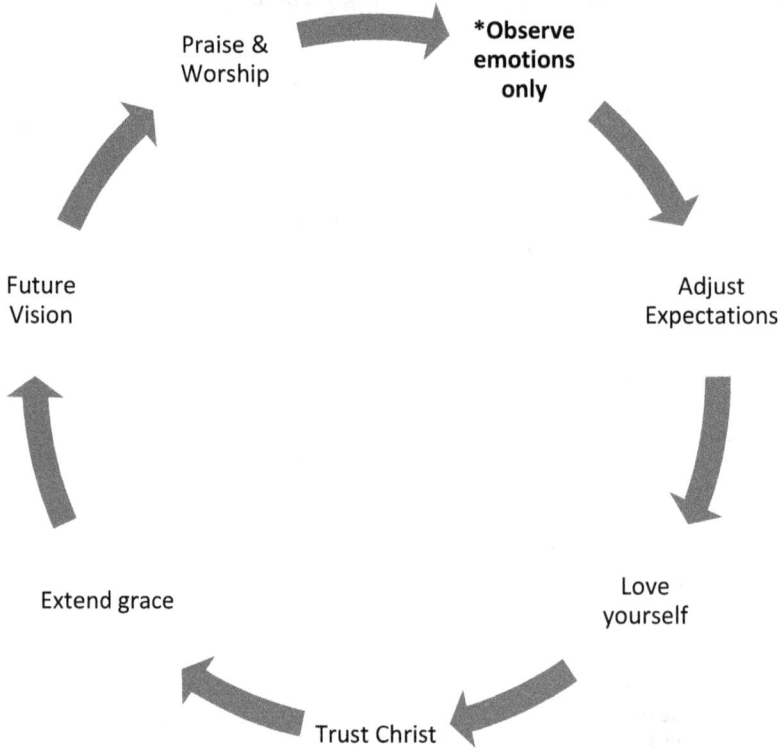

Praise & Worship → *Observe emotions only → Adjust Expectations → Love yourself → Trust Christ → Extend grace → Future Vision → Praise & Worship

Lesson

1) A) **Triggered** - Whenever something triggers us, we have subconscious memory patterns that dictate our responses. We have to intentionally change those patterns.

B) **Observe emotions only** - Recognize emotions are exaggerated and painful, pull them into your consciousness and move them outside of yourself and observe them.

Emotional Movement Quiz
What is this emotion teaching me?
Does something need changed in my life?
Do I get stuck in this emotion often?   When did this emotion first become dominant in my life?
Is there a certain person or circumstance that triggers this emotion?

2) A) **Disappointed** - Unmet expectations can dredge up a whole host of exaggerated emotions. Recognize this and categorize it as a disappointment and not a failure.

B) **Adjust Expectations** – Acceptance is a good place to be. It stops all grieving and striving.

3) A) **Feeling Unloved** – Many times neglect, or abuse has ingrained in us a false belief that we are unloved.

B) **Love yourself** – The truth is *"I have loved you with an everlasting love; I have drawn you with loving-kindness"*. *(Jeremiah 31:3)* Find others that are safe to love and especially invest in loving children. *Love is patient. Love is kind. 1 Corinthians 13:4* If you aren't patient and kind to yourself, of course, you don't feel loved. Stop beating yourself up!

4) A) **Lacking Confidence** – Take the focus off yourself.

B) **Trust Christ** – *Trust in the Lord with all your heart and lean not on your own understanding. (Proverbs 3:5)*

5) A) **Rehearsing Old Wounds** – Old wounds keep us feeling injured. *So, my spirit grows faint within me; my heart within me is dismayed. Psalm 143:4*

B) **Extends Grace** – Be gracious to the weaker parts of yourself. *But where sin increased, grace increased all the more...Romans 5:20*

6) A) **Condemns Self** – What would it look like to be patient and kind with yourself? Make gentleness with yourself a habit.
   B) **Future Vision**- *Where there is no vision, the people perish. Proverbs 29:18*

7) A) **Stuck** – When you feel lame, look up Jesus is coming. *I have no one to help me into the pool when the water is stirred. While I am trying to get in, someone else goes down ahead of me. Jesus said to him, "Get up! Pick up your mat and walk." John 5:7-8*
   B) **Praise & Worship** Often there is nothing we can do about a situation or dire circumstance, so let's just offer to God the sacrifice of our praise. *Through Jesus, therefore, let us continually offer to God a sacrifice of praise—the fruit of lips that openly profess his name. Hebrews 13:15*

Exercise
Analyze your emotional patterns? Are they sober?

Principle
You can't rise higher than your emotions.

Application
Becoming sober emotionally isn't easy, it is a wrestling match with your inner self. It is a acknowledging the emotions and observing them, learning from them and releasing them to God as your sacrifice. This is a conscious choice. This is strict training of your emotions. The key is to keep your emotions under subjection to the Word of God just like Paul did his body. *Everyone who competes in the games goes into strict training... Therefore, I do not run like a man running aimlessly; I do not fight like a man beating the air. No, I beat my body and make it a slave so that after I have preached to others, I myself will not be disqualified for the prize. I Corinthians 9:25-27*

Conclusion

Never do anything illegal, immoral, or unethical. Stand firm, do not cave into peer pressure or emotionally regressive behaviors. If you do, you will be drunk with immature emotions. Instead, preach to yourself. Guard your heart from foolish thinking. *Above all else, guard your heart, for it is the wellspring of life. Proverbs 4:23* This is a wrestling match. Move toxic thoughts out of your head or they will lead to toxic emotions that will hinder your recovery. Now go and enjoy your day!

The Lord is my rock, and my fortress, and my deliverer; my God, my strength in whom I trust; my buckler, and the horn of my salvation, and my higher tower. Psalm 18:2

Almighty God help us to stop drinking from addictive toxic emotions and to drink deeply from the water of life that out of our bellies may flow rivers of living waters to give hope to a desperate and dying world. In Jesus name we pray, Amen. *He that believes on me, as the Scripture has said, out of his belly shall flow rivers of living water. John 7 :38*

Forgiveness
Lesson 11

Introduction

Self-pity, resentment, bitterness, and hatred are prison bars. Forgiveness is the key. So, you say, some people don't deserve forgiveness. I agree, they don't. But you aren't doing it to set them free, but to set yourself free.

Lesson

1) **No excuses.** Sometimes there is no way to pardon or rationalize an offense. We have to just let it go.

2) **Name your offender.** Is this person safe to confront? Will it do any good?

3) **Find Compassion.** Hurting people wound others. This does not condone their actions, but it may help you develop compassion.

4) **Seek out and ask for forgiveness from others.** We all need forgiveness at different points in our lives.

5) **Resolve to not allow an offense to control your thinking or behavior.**

6) **Release all bitterness, anger, and resentment.** Often, I can't resolve my bitterness, I just have to sacrifice it to God and let it go.

7) **Recognize self-pity as unresolved bitterness.**

8) **Don't hold a grudge. Pray for your enemy.** This releases you.

Exercise

Learn what forgiveness is not.

What Forgiveness is Not!
1) It is not approval or justification of a wrong action.
2) It is not making excuses for rebellion or wickedness.
3) It is not reconciliation.
4) It is not denying what they did to us.
5) It is not forgetting what happened.
6) It is not acting like you are not hurt.

7) It does not mean you will not hold them accountable for wrong actions.

Principle

Forgiveness releases me from mental bondage.

Application

Forgiveness Steps
1) Obey the Lord and purpose in your own heart to forgive. This is done out of obedience, not because we feel like it. *Then Peter came to Jesus and asked, "Lord, how many times shall I forgive my brother when he sins against me? Up to seven times? Jesus answered, "I tell you, not seven times, but seventy-seven times." Matthew 18:21-22*
2) Do this every time bitterness is felt. It may be something that needs repeated 100 times until you feel release. This is how you do it: "Lord, there is that bitterness again, I forgive, help me to completely forgive." **Forgiveness is a supernatural work bigger than us.**
3) When forgiveness is almost done, we may feel numb, not care and not think about it anymore. But if you hear yourself saying: "What goes around, comes around," you still have work to do. There is still a hidden root of bitterness keeping you in bondage. *...For out of the overflow of his heart his mouth speaks. Luke 6:45*
4) When you hear something good has happened to them and you rejoice, **forgiveness is complete.** *Love your enemies and pray for those who persecute you that you may be sons of your Father in heaven. Matthew 5:44-45*

Caution
1) Do not go back to ask forgiveness when it would set you up for more abuse.
2) Do not assume responsibility for the outcomes of someone else's poor choices.

3) Do not go back when it would open old wounds for the other person or make things worse.
4) Do not go back and expect the other person to own their offenses and repent to you.
In these situations, go to an accountability partner and obtain good counsel and work through forgiveness or confession.

Conclusion

There was once a man who owed a master ten thousand talents. The king wanted to settle his accounts and called for the man to be brought to him. When the man could not pay, the master ordered <u>him, his wife and children</u> to be sold to repay the debt. The man fell to his knees and asked for patience and another opportunity to pay him back. The master had mercy upon the servant and forgave him the entire debt. But this same servant went out and found a man that owed him a hundred denarii. He grabbed him and choked him and demanded payment. The fellow servant fell to his knees and begged for patience and an opportunity to repay the debt. The unmerciful servant (who had just been forgiven more than he could have ever paid) demanded payment and threw the man in prison. When the master heard the story of the unmerciful servant, he turned him over to the jailers to be tormented until he should pay back all he owed. *Matthew 18:23-34*

This is how my heavenly Father will treat each of you unless you forgive your brother from your heart. Matthew 18:35

The Lord is my rock, and my fortress, and my deliverer; my God, my strength in whom I will trust; my buckler, and the horn of my salvation, and my high tower. Psalm 18:2

Pray Together:
Our Father in heaven,
Hallowed be your name,
Your kingdom come,
Your will be done on earth
*   as it is in heaven.*

Give us today our daily bread.
Forgive us our debts,
    as we also have forgiven our debtors.
And lead us not into temptation
    but deliver us from the evil one. Matthew 6:9-13

Number one reason to forgive:
Matthew 6:14-15 For if you forgive men when they sin against you, your heavenly Father will also forgive you. But if you do not forgive men their sins, your Father will not forgive your sins.

Freedom
Lesson 12

Introduction

True Freedom is the power of self-determination to command your own internal world by intentionally directing all your speech and actions. Develop this maturity skill by starting small. *Whoever can be trusted with very little can be trusted with much, and whoever is dishonest with very little will also be dishonest with much. Luke 16:10KJV* Discipline yourself in small areas of life. Govern and manage the smaller things in life and greater things will be easier to command. The opposite is also true. If you are dishonest in the little things, you will also be dishonest in the greater things. Decide what you will and will not say, think, or do. Start with one area of your life and build on it. Now, make a sovereign choice on how you will live.

Lesson

1) **Mind**-Delve deep into the power of concentration. Reign in your thoughts and tell yourself what you will and will not think. When your passive thoughts wander, take authority and change them to thoughts you want to think. When there are difficult things that you need to think about, think on them until you follow the thinking pattern to the end. If there is no solution or resolution, let it go. Brooding over traumatic memories or painful circumstances are of no help. Recognize any fretting and stop it! If you have thought a tormenting thought a hundred times with no conclusion, then don't let it start. Practice detaching and releasing it. *Set your mind on things above, not on earthly things. Colossians 3:2*

2) **Body**-Arise each morning and purpose to smile. Be in control of when you awaken and go to sleep. Keep a schedule. Allow for flexibility, you don't want anything legalistic. Discipline eating habits, don't go back for seconds. Don't eat late at night. Follow the serving size on the package. Make yourself some general rules that would fit into your lifestyle. Physical activity is vital to a healthy body. If you aren't exercising, it is a marvelous way to detox your thoughts and calm your mind. Here is what the apostle Paul says, *"I therefore so run, not as uncertainty; so fight I, not as one that*

beats the air: but I keep under my body, and bring it into subjection: lest that by any means, when I have preached to others, I myself should be a castaway." 1 Corinthians 9:27KJV

3) **Position**-Christianity is not rights, but righteousness. It is honor and not equality. It is more concerned about what one owes than what is owed. *Be devoted to one another in brotherly love, honor one another above yourselves. Romans 12:10* We are under authority at all times. Authority is a safety net of protection. We are under the laws of the land, government, parents, teachers, employers, ministers, elders, or priest. *Everyone must submit himself to the governing authorities, for there is no authority except that which God has established. The authorities that exist have been established by God. Romans 13:1*

4) **Time**-If we are frustrated, frantic and hassled our time hasn't been ordered by the Lord. Worry is a fruitless time waster and robs us of the pleasure of singing and thanksgiving. Set aside a quiet time every day to meditate on the goodness of the Lord and allow Him to direct your path. Offering to God the first portion of our time consecrates our day for His glory. **Learn to accept disappointments on the one hand and simultaneously joy on the other.** If we are unable to lift our disappointments up to God with a sacrifice of praise, time will be robbed with fretfulness and fear. Learn the wisdom of Solomon. *There is a time for everything, and a season for every activity under the heavens: a time to be born and a time to die, a time to plant and a time to uproot, a time to kill and a time to heal, a time to tear down and a time to build, a time to weep and a time to laugh, a time to mourn and a time to dance, a time to scatter stones and a time to gather them, a time to embrace and a time to refrain from embracing, a time to search and a time to give up, a time to keep and a time to throw away, a time to tear and a time to mend, a time to be silent and a time to speak, a time to love and a time to hate, a time for war and a time for peace. Ecclesiastes 3:1*

5) **Possessions**-Everything I possess is a gift from God. *Every good and perfect gift is from above, coming down from the Father of heavenly lights, who does not change like shifting shadows. James 1:17 Freely you have received, freely give. Matthew 10:8* Things are temporal and to be held

loosely. We don't need to hoard. Stewardship is faithful character skill and helps us manage our possessions. *So, we fix our eyes not on what is seen, but on what is unseen. For what is seen is temporary, but what is unseen is eternal. 2 Corinthians 4:18* Everything that is God's is at our disposal. So, do not store up treasures on earth. *Do not store up for yourselves treasures on earth, where moth and rust destroy, and where thieves break in and steal. But store up treasures in heaven, where moth and rust do not destroy, and where thieves do not break in and steal. For where you treasure is, there your heart will be also. Matthew 6:19-21*

6) **Work**-Honorable work is work whether it is a sanitation worker or heart surgeon. *Whatever you do, work at it with all your heart, as working for the Lord, not for me. Colossians 3:23* A sense of duty to care for children, elderly and neighbors brings great joy when it is done with a whole heart of love. Changing diapers, cleaning bathrooms and dishes are an act of service to the Lord. *...whatever you did for one of the least of these brothers of mine, you did for me. Matthew 25:40* The Lord Jesus took a towel and washed the dirty feet of the disciples like a servant. *...he poured water into a basin and began to wash his disciples' feet, drying them with the towel that was wrapped around him. John 13:5* There is no work that is beneath us. If it needs done, do it. The greatest among you is one who serves. *The greatest among you will be your servant. Matthew 23:11*

7) **Emotions**-Just as we take thoughts captive, we must take feelings captive to make them obedient unto Christ. *We demolish arguments and every pretension that sets itself up against the knowledge of God. 2 Corinthians 10:5* Feelings have no intelligence and no intellect. They are like blind guides to lead us into a ditch. Resolve to do what is right. This is a decision of the will, not the emotion. Practice self-mastery over emotions. Feel them. Observe them. Learn from them. Grow from them, but do not indulge them unto weak and moody disposition. *But the fruit of the Spirit is ... self-control. Galatians 5:22-23*

Exercise

Make a list of all your problems and their corresponding emotions. Choose one to focus on this week and take dominion.

Principle
Faithfulness in the little things develops faithfulness in the bigger things.

Application

Make a career out of volunteering to be discipled. Look for mentors. Pray for mentors. Listen carefully for instructions. Athletes and instrumentalist are the happiest students on a campus and are the most disciplined.

Athletes:
1) submit to coaches
2) obey the game rules
3) submit to rigorous training
4) works with a team and
5) submits to a schedule.
He that has no rule over his own spirit is like a city that is broken down and without walls. Proverbs 25:28

Conclusion

Internally controlling your own self is powerful recovery. This is true freedom. This can only come through disciplining yourself according to God's principles and not according to our fickle feelings.

Jesus felt emotions. He was angry at the money changers in the temple. (John 2:14-15) He wept at the tomb of Lazarus. (John 11:35) He experienced anguish of soul unto the point of sweating great drops of blood at the Garden of Gethsemane before the crucifixion. (Luke 22:44) He would have felt rejection, persecution and abandonment at the cross, not to mention the physical torture. But he set himself to do the will of the Father, no matter what! (Matthew 26:36-46)

The Lord is my rock, and my fortress, and my deliverer; my God, my strength in whom I will trust; my buckler, and the horn of my salvation, and my high tower. Psalm 18:2

Father in heaven we bless your name. We thank you for the opportunity to obey your will and not ours. Let us cast our emotions on the altar of sacrifice. Let them be brought under subjection to the Word of God and grant us the self-control to bring every emotion into the obedience of Christ. Let us experience true freedom that we may enjoy a peaceful heart and mind in Christ Jesus our Lord. Amen.

MODERATORS

1) Print pdf from enablersjourney.com website.
2) Open in prayer.
3) Review Group Rules.
4) Review last week's lesson. Ask how they were able to apply it to their life and any success or failures they experienced.
5) Do the audio presentation (YouTube video/Angie G Meadows; or Podcast audio/Rock of Recovery) or teach your own presentation using the material.
6) Go through the lesson one point at a time for open discussion.
7) If group is over 8-12 members, split it up into smaller groups for discussion. Train your stronger believers for co-leader support positions.
8) Give examples of how God helped you solve the problem.
9) End the group in prayer (Take prayer request or have a basket for them to write out written request and ask them to mark the request "private" or "public").
10) If time allows, add an opportunity for those with heavy burdens to stay longer for encouragement and prayer.

SMALL GROUP RULES

1) Give everyone an opportunity to speak.
2) Keep the discussion to the topic.
3) We are not here to "fix" each other. We are here to support and encourage one another.
4) If you do not want to share, simply say "pass" when it comes to your turn.
5) It is vital that this is a safe place for everyone. No negative, judgmental, or condemning comments. The Rule is LOVE!
6) Confidentiality is mandatory and is taken very seriously.
7) Whatever is spoken in this room, stays in this room.
8) If during the week, you discuss another member's comments among one another, it is to be in the spirit of prayer and encouragement and not in mockery or ridicule. No gossiping or slandering will be tolerated.
9) There will be a release of anyone who wants to leave after the lesson and discussion time.
10) There will often be added extra time of sharing at the end of the group for those with heavy burdens who want to share their struggles and receive individual prayer or for those who want to stay and encourage those struggling.

LEADERSHIP GUIDELINES

Dishonorable Leadership	Honorable Leadership
Anger	Happy Countenance
Use of fear tactics	Approachable
Threats/Bullying	Patient and Kind
Retaliation for being confronted	Gracious; holds others accountable
Hasty/Rash	Treats everyone the same
Impatient	Good self-identity
Arrogant	Good boundaries
Values self, money or project goals more than others	Good mentors Good relationships
Holds a grudge	Unemotional decision maker
Plays favorites	Leads through serving
Casts confusion on situations to blame shift	Humble- Leads with power and under submission to his authority
Makes emotional decisions not principally based decisions	Will do what is right, no matter the consequences
Denies problems	Good listener
Deals only with superficial problems	Forgives easily; coaches weaker ones; encourages others.
Ignores the main problem	Identifies root problems
Does not seek counsel	Seek many counselors
Ask impossible things	Able to plan and develop goals
Unrealistic/Demanding	Able to follow through with a plan
*Adapted from observation of the behaviors of Nebuchadnezzar the pagan king in the book of Daniel.	Always same level of emotional availability

Rules: No bullying or verbal abuse ever!
Kind, but firm!

GOOD FOLLOWER

1. Respects Authority
2. Protects Good Name
3. Learns to Stand Alone (not follow a crowd)
4. Guards the truth
5. Takes responsibility for actions
6. Honorable and fair in decisions
7. Makes good sound financial decisions
8. Lives with Self-Control
9. Moderation in all things
10. Gives good days work without complaint
11. Always on time; dependable
12. Never gossips, slanders, or accuses
13. Takes any issues up the ladder through the chain of command
14. Guards all that is entrusted into their hands; trustworthy
15. Refuses to do anything illegal, unethical, or immoral

*You must learn to be a good follower to be a good leader.

AUTHOR'S BIOGRAPHIES

Angie G. Meadows graduated from St Mary's School of Nursing as a Registered Nurse, Marshall University with a Bachelor's in Nursing and Ohio State University with a Master's in Nursing. She has worked at multiple hospitals in multiple capacities. Angie has been a keen observer of human behaviors as she has dealt with enablers and many with Substance Use Disorder over the years. She is currently a wife, mother, grandmother, speaker, and writer. Her favorite pastime is quilting.

Sarah J Meadows graduated from Liberty University with a bachelor's degree in psychology. She has worked in the public-school system as a Therapeutic Day Treatment Counselor. She is currently pursuing a master's degree in clinical Mental Health Counseling. Sarah enjoys her friends and her beloved corgi.

OTHER RESOURCES BY THE AUTHORS

A Thousand Tears: An Enabler's Journey ISBN 9781732810204

https://www.amazon.com/Thousand-Tears-Enablers-Journey/dp/1732810206

This is the same book as Enabler's Journey: A Christian Perspective, but it is written with principles and not Scriptures.

The book identifies the Enabler's Cycle and our conflict with individuals with addiction. Identifying manipulative, devouring, or toxic relationships in our life and learning to confront and detach. This book is a useful tool in dealing with person's with Substance Use Disorder or abusive loved ones. It also includes multiple self-assessment tools: Enabler's paradigm, entanglement gauge, anxiety quotient, trust scales, and much more.

An Enabler's Journey: A Christian Perspective ISBN: 9781732810211

https://read.amazon.com/kp/embed?asin=B07KDK1L1F&preview=newtab&linkCode=kpe&ref_=cm_sw_r_kb_dp_aaEgFbPSB9P11 Book preview.

https://www.amazon.com/Enablers-Journey-Christian-Perspective-ebook/dp/B07KDK1L1F/ref=pd_sim_351_2/147-3762080-9342150?_encoding=UTF8&pd_rd_i=B07KDK1L1F&pd_rd_r=58dcb7aa-921e-4665-b6f0-ce42ced569ff&pd_rd_w=fau3o&pd_rd_wg=wWRbM&pf_rd_p=6f740e39-0c25-4380-8008-7a4156dab959&pf_rd_r=3W4KGCECXB8C6AVDAQJ0&psc=1&refRID=3W4KGCECXB8C6AVDAQJ0

This book is 300+ pages and 24 chapters. It is almost the same book as *A Thousand Tear: An Enabler's Journey* except it has a 100+ Scriptures to validate the principles for dealing with difficult people in relationships.

Enabler's Journey Recovery Plan: Enabler's Journey Recovery Series: Book 1 ISBN: 9781732810228

https://www.amazon.com/Enablers-Journey-Recovery-Plan-Book-ebook/dp/B07NTND743/ref=sr_1_1?dchild=1&keywords=angie+g+meadows&qid=1590167957&s=books&sr=1-

This is a 100+ page Book One of a recovery workbook series. It guides individuals and clients to understand enabling behaviors and evaluate their current participation in perpetuating a person with Substance Use Disorder's illness. The enabler will learn to recognize the cycle of enabling, entanglement, excuses and beliefs that handicap an enabler from recovery. It also coaches in the courage needed for detaching from destructive people and circumstances we cannot control. The book includes an enabler's recovery plan, accountability questionnaire, self-care program and a plan for identifying unhealthy and healthy coping strategies. It will also guide the recovering enabler to determine a level of safe involvement with a person with Substance Use Disorder and how to identify true and false recovery, rebuild trust, and avoid the snare of another enabling relationship. It will help us recognize dysfunctional thinking and our false belief system that keeps us entangled. There are 5 chapters from the original *A Thousand Tears: An Enabler's Journey* book and 3 extra in-depth recovery chapters and many added self-evaluation charts. This is a beginner book or small group book for an Enablers. It is short and concise with lots of diagrams and easy to understand flowcharts. It is a great beginner tool with lots of reflective questions for counsellors or small groups to use in guiding enablers to recovery.

Enabler's Journey Detachment: Enabler's Journey Recovery Series Book 2 ISBN: 9781732810235

https://www.amazon.com/Enablers-Journey-Detachment-Recovery-Book-ebook/dp/B07RQWP5YR/ref=sr_1_fkmr0_2?dchild=1&keywords=angie+g+meadows+detachment&qid=1590168176&s=digital-text&sr=1-2-fkmr0

This book empowers us to learn survival skills with 12 DETACHMENT PRINCIPLES. The spiralling financial consequences, mental anguish, emotional chaos, and physical drain of enabling begs the voice of detachment to ensure self-preservation. This book is a useful tool in dealing with Substance Use Disorder, or other individuals with abusive or irresponsible behaviors. It includes many self-assessment tools: Entitlement Evaluation, Empowerment Plan, Helpless Trap, Healthier Me, Healthy Speech Evaluation, Negative Emotional Triggers, Unmet Needs, Obsessive Thinking Traps, Forgiveness, Bitterness, Reconciliation, Holidays, Suffering, Power to Stop Enabling, Self-Talk, Rules for Survival, practical steps, reflective thinking and much, much more.

Rock of Recovery Defeating Anxiety: Christian Enabler/Addiction Recovery Book

https://www.amazon.com/Rock-Recovery-Anxiety-Trap-Christian/dp/1732810249

Painful emotions drive toxic relationships and addictive behaviors. Developmental emotional maturity skills mimic physical developmental skills. As a child grows physically, they learn to roll over, sit up, crawl, walk and then run. The development of emotions can be stunted or undeveloped and need to be matured and nurtured through intentional training and disciplining our intellect and thinking to support, nurture and master our emotions. Conquering anxiety, finding a safe self internally, learning to break a helpless/victim trap with disciplined thinking, uncovering hidden emotions under the cloak of anxiety, overcoming double-mindedness and internally finding rest and peace are just a few developmental emotional skills to rule and reign over our internal world.

Rule and Reign your Internal World: Defeating Anxiety
Youth/Adult Emotional Maturity Skills

https://www.amazon.com/Rule-Reign-Your-Internal-World/dp/1732810257/ref=sr_1_1?dchild=1&keywords=Rule+and+reign+your+internal+world&qid=1602527688&s=books&sr=1-1

Ruling and Reigning our internal world through developmental emotional maturity skills halts toxic emotions that cause anxiety. This emotional ability mimics physical developmental skills. As a child grows physically, they learn to roll over, sit up, crawl, walk and then run. The development of emotions can be stunted or undeveloped and need to be matured and nurtured through intentional training and disciplining our intellect and thinking to support, nurture and master our emotions. Conquering anxiety, finding a safe self internally, learning to break a helpless/victim trap with disciplined thinking, uncovering hidden emotions under the cloak of anxiety, overcoming double-mindedness and internally finding rest and peace are just a few developmental emotional skills to rule and reign over our internal world. Defeating Anxiety has 12 lessons to practice with 12 principles to learn to govern your thinking. **(This is the same information as the Rock of Recovery Series for Enablers and those with Substance Use Disorder. It is reorganized for anyone needing Developmental Emotional Maturity Skills.)** This series is an individual devotional, home-school, or Christian School curriculum, Family Devotions, or Small Group anxiety study.

www.ingramcontent.com/pod-product-compliance
Lightning Source LLC
Chambersburg PA
CBHW060145050426
42448CB00010B/2307